Original title:
Rootbound Revelations

Copyright © 2025 Creative Arts Management OÜ
All rights reserved.

Author: Dorian Ashford
ISBN HARDBACK: 978-1-80581-732-1
ISBN PAPERBACK: 978-1-80581-259-3
ISBN EBOOK: 978-1-80581-732-1

Harmonies of the Hidden

In a pot too small for dreams to roam,
A cactus hums, feeling right at home,
Sipping sunlight, laughing at the space,
Poking fun at every passing face.

Worms tap-dance in a soil parade,
While daisies gossip in the shade,
"Hey, did you hear what the fern just said?"
"Yeah, but you know he's a little green in the head!"

Under the earth, the roots intertwine,
Sharing secrets over sips of brine,
"My flowers bloom better than yours," they boast,
"Let's throw a roots party, we'll have a toast!"

A tulip winks, its petals all aglow,
"Let's plant some jokes, watch them grow!"
The daisies chuckle, "That's quite the tease,
Let's dig up some laughter, we'll plant it with ease!"

When Time Stands Still

Clock ticks slow, like molasses,
Every tick a silly face.
Time's a jester in its castle,
Bouncing on a rubber base.

Days blend in a wobbly line,
Like spaghetti on a fork.
Laughing at this playful sign,
Twirling time, a wacky stork.

Gnarled Truths

Silly knots in tangled thoughts,
Growling like a grumpy tree.
Truth's a game that laughter caught,
Twisted points of comedy.

Round and round, the branches swing,
Poking fun at life, it's true.
Each gnarled grin makes my heart sing,
Nature's jesters, quite the crew.

Shrouded in Green

Hidden under leafy laughs,
Where shadows dance, and giggles bloom.
Lizards on their leafy paths,
Tickling air with playful zoom.

Frogs in suits of emerald hue,
Debating how to catch a fly.
In their cryptic world, who knew?
Nature's humor flutters by.

The Roots of Memory

Buried deep in silly sights,
Memories sprout with leafy cheer.
Each twist and turn, the funny bites,
Nostalgic roots tangled near.

Laughter greets each creeping vine,
Whispers of the past unwind.
In this garden, joy's the sign,
Where playful specters you will find.

Ties That Bind

In the garden, weeds hold hands,
With old shoes, they form funky bands.
Carrots gossip about the sun,
While potatoes laugh, 'This is fun!'

Daisies tell tales of the breeze,
As onions dance, oh, what a tease!
The turnips chuckle, 'We can't hide,'
Together, they thrive, side by side.

Roots of Knowing

Beneath the soil, secrets creep,
A radish whispers, 'I can't sleep.'
The brussel sprouts roll their eyes,
While chicory dreams of the skies.

They jest about old-fashioned soil,
And stick together, through thick and toil.
With laughter loud, they share their fate,
In tangled fun, they celebrate.

Veins of the Forest

In the woods, squirrels slice and dice,
Finding acorns with a bit of spice.
A raccoon wears a mask so neat,
While trees giggle, 'What a treat!'

Leaves chat about the autumn's chill,
With pinecones plotting mischief still.
Together they twist, turn, and sway,
Enjoying each snicker of the day.

Elements of Our Past

Old rocks reminisce of days gone by,
As dust bunnies shrug and just sigh.
The river chuckles, 'I've seen it all!'
While standing stones stand proud and tall.

Air swirls tales like a playful breeze,
While fire flickers, 'Let's tease the trees!'
Earth grumbles softly about the mess,
But all agree, it's just finesse.

Secrets that Cling to the Ground

In a garden where gnomes gossip loud,
The carrots chuckle, feeling quite proud.
Potatoes complain, trapped in their hole,
While radishes plot to steal the whole role.

The daisies dance in a flowered jam,
Hiding secrets, giggling like a sham.
Under the soil, the worms weave a show,
With tales of the dirt, they know more than you know.

The Embrace of Twisted Fates

The vines tangle in a wild embrace,
While bushes around can't keep up the pace.
A fern dreams of travel, to root and to roam,
But finds itself wedged in its leafy old home.

The ivy laughs as it climbs to the moon,
While daisies complain, 'This will end very soon!'
Twisted all over, the roots wear a grin,
In this garden circus, let the fun begin!

Nature's Confessions in the Shade

Under the oak, in a sun-drenched spot,
The squirrels hold secrets, they've tied up in knots.
A flower spills tea on the gossiping breeze,
While ants cart off crumbs like they're on a spree.

"Did you see that tree?" whispers one to the next,
"It's shedding some bark; I guess it feels vexed!"
A butterfly giggles and flutters on by,
While whispers of dirt make the daisies sigh.

Renewal in the Thicket's Grasp

In the thicket where thorns hold tight,
A berry bursts forth, what a wonderful sight!
"Excuse me," it shouts, "I'm sweet as can be,
Trapped in this tangle, come celebrate me!"

The bushes all chuckle, "Next party is grand,
You'll have to wear thorns if you want a hand!"
Yet laughter erupts in this thorny attire,
For the joy of the wild will never expire.

Treasuring the Tangles

In a pot that feels quite snug,
Plants gather like a cozy hug.
Leaves twist like they're doing a dance,
Whispers of soil, oh what a chance!

Grapevines giggle, a leafy parade,
Talking of sunshine and cool shade.
They plot to stretch, escape their space,
But for now, they're stuck in this place.

Dreams of the Earthbound

Little seeds dream of the sky,
Wishing they could learn to fly.
But every root's a lazy chap,
Too comfy in this earthen lap.

The daisies chat, "We're stuck in this mud!
What if we break free, just like a flood?"
But they laugh hard, their bloom's a delight,
Who needs the sky when you're jolly and bright?

Butterflies Beneath the Bark

Underneath the old oak's skin,
A monarch waits, ready to spin.
"Can these branches hold such grace?
Let's hope I fit in this small space!"

Bugs debate who's the best at fly,
While ants march by with a sigh.
"Why dream of flying when we're this grand?
We'll rule the ground, a solid plan!"

Sanctuary in Shadows

In the shade where the tall weeds play,
Creatures gather, spinning tales all day.
"Why chase the light? It's much too bright!
We're more fabulous in this dim light!"

A toadstool grand hosts a chat so sweet,
While fireflies blink like a disco beat.
Who needs the sun? We shine right here,
In our cozy nook, we have no fear!

The Language of Wistful Plants

In leafy whispers, secrets dwell,
Cabbage winks, can you hear it tell?
Tomatoes chuckle, with a juicy grin,
While the peas debate who'll win the spin.

Sunflowers strut, they're quite the show,
Dancing happily in the sun's warm glow.
Cacti gossip, prickly and spry,
Exchanging tales of the clouds in the sky.

Nourished by the Timidity of Touch

A gentle caress, the fern holds its breath,
While daisies giggle at their quaint little heft.
Spinach squints under clumsy hands,
Saying, 'Do be careful, we have plans!'

Sassy ivy climbs up the wall,
Hoping no one takes a fateful fall.
Even roots stretch, feeling quite bold,
But secretly cracking jokes, untold.

Hidden Harmonies of the Deep

Beneath the soil where the shadows play,
The carrots make music in a subterranean way.
Radishes hum tunes of joyful cheer,
While buried beetroot whisper, 'We're here!'

Mushrooms sway to a cash crop beat,
Sending spores dancing, all lively and neat.
A harmony brewed from the damp, dark ground,
With roots as the drummers, it's laughter they found.

Stories of Stems and Silent Shadows

Tall stems have tales of the winds they've braved,
While silent shadows dance, so shrewdly saved.
Bamboo stretches, laughing at fate,
As daisies contend who's better on a date.

Whimsical leaves in the softest breeze,
Fanning tall tales, like gossip from trees.
In a patch of green where antics unfold,
The wildest stories are silently told.

Tendrils of Time

In a pot too small, the plant does whine,
"I can't stretch out! My leaves entwine!"
The sun's a tease, the rain's a trick,
"Oh let me grow! I need a kick!"

With every wiggle, roots do sigh,
"Is it too much to ask? Just let me fly!"
They plan a heist, a daring dive,
"We'll break this pot! We'll feel alive!"

Messages in the Moss

Beneath the shade, the moss does speak,
"Hey there, fella, it's time to sneak!"
They scribble notes on leaves so sleek,
"Join the fun! You've hit your peak!"

With squishy feet, they start to roll,
"It's a slippery world, let's take a stroll!"
They giggle loud, the forest glares,
"We're just on a mission, catching air!"

The Unfolding Mystery

A bud looked up, perplexed and shy,
"Is it me or is time flying high?"
The petals whispered, "Take a chance,
Let your colors burst, join the dance!"

A flower peeped, with paint so bold,
"I'm tired of secrets, let's be told!"
The garden erupted, a riot of hue,
"Who knew our lives were a circus too?"

Half-Told Stories

In the shade, the tales are spun,
"I fought a beast! It weighed a ton!"
The gnome just laughed, a knowing grin,
"You tripped on roots, that's where you've been!"

With every twist, a yarn grows tall,
"I climbed a tree to rescue a squirrel!"
But with a slip and a flop and a fall,
"It rescued you! Didn't you recall?"

Through Loamy Layers

In the garden, worms do dance,
Chasing rays of sun by chance.
They giggle, twist, and wiggle here,
In their deep, earthy pioneer.

With every scoop, a story's found,
Shovel's humor knows no bounds.
A beetle tells a joke so grand,
As dandelions take a stand.

When the Ground Speaks

Oh listen close to soil's lore,
It whispers tales of roots galore.
Crickets chirp in pun-filled glee,
While moles plan their comedy spree.

The daisies laugh, the grass takes sides,
As earthworms launch their joke-filled rides.
A talking stone with wise old cracks,
Shares puns about these hidden tracks.

Stories in the Twisted Trunks

Old trees twist, in knots they joke,
Each branch a punchline's gentle poke.
Squirrels chuckle, scurry with zest,
Their acorn tales are simply the best.

With every ring, a riddle hides,
Laughter echoes in woodsy tides.
The bark confesses with a wink,
That roots have secrets too — just think!

Depths of the Unknown

Digging deep, I find a shoe,
What else lies hidden, who knew?
A lost sock tells me how it felt,
While ancient bones rise from the silt.

The gopher shrieks, "It's not mine!"
As treasure hunters squabble and whine.
Each layer peeled, a laugh unfolds,
Beneath the surface, joy never grows old.

Tangled Truths Beneath the Surface

In a garden where veggies like to play,
Lettuce whispers secrets, they think won't stray.
Carrots giggle, buried in the dirt,
Cheerful potatoes poke, with a little hurt.

Old weeds gossip, think they're so wise,
While mushrooms roll their spore-filled eyes.
But under the ground, what chaos unfolds,
As radishes argue about their bold holds.

A raccoon steals snacks, thinking he's sly,
While brussels sprouts wait for a good pie.
Shovels and rakes come to disrupt the fun,
But roots keep their secrets, just on the run.

So here's to the garden, absurd and kooky,
Where veggies unite, get all broody and spooky.
With tangled truths lurking just out of sight,
The shenanigans flourish, oh what a delight!

Secrets of the Silent Soil

Beneath the soil, where the dark things dwell,
Worms share tales they know far too well.
Dirt has a history, some laugh and some cry,
As ants plan a coup, oh so sly!

There's a party of seeds, dreaming to grow,
Jumping with glee as the wind starts to blow.
"Who's sprouting first?" they giggle and cheer,
While the wise old oak pretends not to hear.

Rocks grumble loudly, tired of the wait,
As grasses tease roots about their fate.
The earth has its puzzles, its giggle-filled truths,
Hiding in shadows, like cheeky old sleuths.

From moles in their tunnels, to bugs on a spree,
All trying to claim the most cozy degree.
Secrets abound in the soil's embrace,
Where whispers grow louder in this zany space!

Whispers from the Earth's Embrace

Oh listen closely, there's chatter and mirth,
From the ticklish roots dancing beneath the earth.
They trade comical stories of frost and of rain,
While the daisies break out into spontaneous refrain.

Raccoons are the judges of every seed's plight,
Critiquing the shovels, they giggle all night.
The sun teases flowers, "Are you ready to shine?"
As turtlenecks ponder if spring's too divine.

Worms put on plays about soil and slime,
Each wiggle and jiggle, a step out of line.
Potatoes recite rhymes as they sit in their patch,
And garlic's the pun master, always on the catch.

With roots intertwined in a silly ballet,
The earth giggles softly, come join in the play!
For in its embrace, there's laughter galore,
In the underground circus, you'll always want more!

Beneath the Canopy of Dreams

In the shade of the trees where the funny things hide,
Nuts tell tall tales, swell with nutty pride.
Leaves wiggle and dance, casting shadows so deep,
While squirrels recite legends, then giggle and leap.

The roots hold a meeting, on why they are stumped,
Plotting a heist for what humans once dumped.
But the mushrooms, amused, just shake with glee,
As they brew up a potion for all to see.

A bush claims it's wise, full of berries and spice,
While the daisies all chuckle, "Oh really? How nice!"
The canopy whispers, the wind plays along,
As the earth bursts with laughter, nature's own song.

So come and join now in this whimsical tale,
Where laughter finds roots and loves to prevail.
Beneath the green cover, the humor runs free,
A comedy club, as absurd as can be!

Ties of the Forgotten

In a garden where weeds hold a dance,
The flowers all giggle, a comedic romance.
The carrots wear glasses, quite scholarly, you see,
While radishes shout, "You can't grow like me!"

They ponder the gossip of soil and of rain,
The gossip turns wild, driving plants a bit insane.
The tomatoes are blushing, the cucumbers tease,
"We might blend a salad, but you can't dress as peas!"

Uncle Onion is sulking, his layers exposed,
Saying, "Why am I the one always opposed?"
The herbs crack a smile, and the celery bends,
Laughing at roots that just can't make amends.

So in this odd patch, where chaos abounds,
The laughter of greens is the best of all sounds.
Each plant has a story, so silly, so grand,
In ties of the forgotten, they hold each other's hand.

Rebirth in Dark Places

In the shadows reside, some roots with a grin,
They whisper of secrets, they revel in sin.
'What's that peeking in?' asks a shy little sprout,
"It's just the old carrots, trying to creep out!"

They bark at the moon, with a snicker and jig,
While moles in the darkness dance a quick gig.
Rats wearing top hats are sipping their tea,
As beetles debate if they're arty or free.

With a laugh in the dim light, they plot their escape,
From the confines of darkness, like an odd little cape.
They'll wiggle and jive till the sun starts to rise,
In rebirth, they blossom with mischievous ties.

So don't judge these roots with their whimsical flair,
They thrive in the shadows, without any care.
In dark places, the humor just tickles the night,
Their rebirth is a giggle, a most curious sight!

Clarity from the Chaos

In the mess of the mulch, where the oddest things grow,
A garden's a circus, and here's the big show.
The weeds line up wanting a place in the sun,
While daisies are plotting to outshine for fun.

The sunflowers gossip, so tall and so proud,
'We'll bloom like the banners, we'll stand out in a crowd!'
While the carrots beneath don't get any praise,
They're digging their holes, their own humble ways.

A radish remarks, 'Why's life such a race?'
While onions just cry in their own little space.
Yet laughter erupts when the shovels get dropped,
Chaos abounds when a handful is swapped!

Yet amidst all this chaos, a lesson unfolds:
In clarity found, there's a wisdom that holds.
Amongst all the plants, small and tall, make a sound,
It's the humor of growth that forever surrounds!

The Lullaby of Roots

Under the soil, where the giggles reside,
Little roots whisper secrets, they just can't abide.
Dreaming of sunlight and dancing so free,
But they're stuck in the ground, oh dear, what a spree!

The compost is chatting, full of old tales,
While mushrooms are plotting their whimsical gales.
"A lullaby's needed," the weeds start to hum,
While the peonies sigh, "Oh, we'll make it so fun!"

"Let's sing to the rain and the sweet morning dew,
And dream of big gardens where we all can woo!"
As each root settles in for a night filled with cheer,
The lullaby of roots makes their worries disappear.

So if you should wander through the plants in the night,
You might just encounter their laughter and light.
For beneath all the soil, where they wiggle and play,
The lullaby of roots keeps troubles at bay!

Unraveled by the Underground

In the soil, a party starts,
Worms wear hats, and dance with arts.
Beneath the ground, the mischief brews,
Like tiny gnomes in muddy shoes.

Potatoes share their cheesy jokes,
While carrots crack up, laughing folks.
Onions cry, but it's just for fun,
They're not shedding tears, they've just begun.

Beetles hop like disco kings,
With ladybugs that flap their wings.
In this underground soirée grand,
Everyone's here, a merry band.

So next time you see roots below,
Remember, they're putting on a show!
With funky moves and giggling puns,
A hidden world that never shuns.

Entwined Echoes of the Heart

Two vines twist in a playful race,
Trying to win the heart of space.
With giggles soft and playful sighs,
They tangle up, then switch the ties.

They whisper dreams to the sleepy ground,
In unison, their laugh is sound.
A contest starts of who can bend,
But in the end, both just pretend.

A tangled mess, yet so divine,
Their wriggly love is a funny line.
Each twist and turn tells a tale,
Of leafy hearts that never pale.

So if you see them laugh and play,
Know that love can be a ballet.
In the garden's light, they truly shine,
With echoes sweet that intertwine.

Hidden Currents of Growth

In the garden, a wiggle's found,
A celery stalk runs underground.
It tells a tale of silly fights,
With peas and beans on silly nights.

Radishes play hide and seek,
While sweet potatoes play peek-a-boo peak.
With sprouting glee, they take their place,
In a world of dirt—a vast embrace.

Chasing sunbeams, they laugh and stretch,
In mud so thick, it's quite the sketch.
With roots that dance, they wiggle about,
A hidden current that leaves no doubt.

So next time you plant that tiny seed,
Remember the fun in every deed.
In the soil, there's a party to know,
Where life sprouts up in joyful flow.

The Dance of Forgotten Tendrils

Beneath the leaves, a dance goes on,
Tendrils twirl from dusk to dawn.
They sway with rhythm, twist and twine,
In a leafy world where sunbeams shine.

Old friends gather without a care,
Whispering tales, braiding through air.
With laughter loud and wiggles fierce,
Each tendril's tale, they love to pierce.

Over rocks and roots they prance,
Taking every chance to enhance.
A silly waltz, a funky groove,
In this green ballet, they always move.

So if you peek beneath the green,
You'll find a world like you've never seen.
With forgotten friends and giggles bright,
Their tales of joy are quite the sight.

Awakenings in the Enclosed Wild

In a pot so snug and tight,
A sprout wakes up in morning light.
Said, "Am I in a fancy jail?"
Turns out, it's a plant's fairytale!

With a sprinkle here, a nudge on ground,
Dreams of sprawling all around.
Craving space and skies so vast,
But stuck with a friend, the gardening cast!

Whispers of blooms and colorful cheer,
While dodging the cat that prowls near.
"Can I grow wings or just a vine?"
"Guess I'll ask the worms for a sign!"

Chasing sunbeams, oh what a race,
In my little patch, I'll find my space!
Though pot-bound, I dance and sway,
Celebrating growth in my own quirky way!

Resilience Among the Sticks and Stones

Amidst the rocks and tangled weeds,
A daisy dreams of sunlit deeds.
"This ground is tough, but so am I,"
"I'll bloom where clods refuse to die!"

A ladybug rolls by and grins,
"You're tougher than my spider friends!"
"Oh please, I'm not afraid of mud,"
"Just try to drown my roots in flood!"

With every storm that shakes the leaves,
The daisies giggle, here's their thieves:
A dozen weeds play dress-up, too,
"Together, we can rule this view!"

A pact is made among the pins,
To dance through rain and laugh at sins.
In this chaos, beauty grows,
Resilience shines where nobody knows!

The Veins of the Verdant Realm

In the soil of secrets, roots entwine,
With whispers of a grapevine's whine.
"Can you hear me?" shouts a tiny sprout,
"Tell the world what I'm about!"

Through tangled fibers, stories creep,
Of outdoor parties, soil so deep.
"Let's plan a bash beneath the sun,"
"Where rabbits free and gophers run!"

The murmurs of cells weave tales untold,
Of hilarious dreams, both shy and bold.
"You think you're stuck? Just wiggle a bit!"
"Dancing roots in a perfect fit!"

Join the revels in leaf and vine,
Where laughter flows like sweetened wine.
In this realm of green's surprise,
Life giggles loud beneath sunny skies!

Echoes of Life in the Loamy Depths

Beneath the surface, a party brews,
With earthworms boasting 'bout their views.
"We have the best dirt for our show!"
"A loamy rave, let's make it glow!"

The beetles bop, the fungi twirl,
"Who needs a crown? Just give me a swirl!"
While roots relay their funny smarts,
"Dirt's where the wildest fun starts!"

A dance-off in the earthy night,
With potatoes claiming, "We're a fright!"
The radishes roll with silly grace,
In the depths of dusk, they find their place!

With laughter echoing 'round the bends,
Celebrating life, the humor sends.
In the heart of loam, such joy's amassed,
In these depths, the memories last!

Silent Musings of the Thicket

In the thicket where whispers dwell,
A shrub thinks it's a magician, oh well!
It conjures up moves from deep underground,
While squirrels play poker without any sound.

A raccoon in a top hat spins tales so grand,
Of acorns so rich from a generous hand.
He juggles three nuts, quite the sight to see,
While a wise old owl hoots, 'Just let it be!'

Beneath the Boughs

Beneath the boughs where shadows trot,
A hedgehog claims he's got a plot.
He's growing a garden of prickly delight,
But only the weeds seem to grow overnight.

The rabbits all giggle, their ears in a flop,
While the hedgehog's schemes seem to never stop.
'Oh, look at my carrots!' he proudly croons,
But they're just old socks with holes like moons!

Tethered to Time

Tethered to time, a worm wrote a book,
On how to avoid a gardening nook.
It's filled with advice on escaping the spade,
But only good for the cake that it made.

The veggies protest, they're ready to flee,
From the salad that looms, what a sight to see!
'We won't be your lunch!' they shout with a cheer,
While the worm just laughs, 'I'm safe—I'm right here!'

Sown in Shadows

Sown in shadows where sunlight forgets,
A cactus declares it's the best at bets.
It wagers its spikes against dandelion fluff,
While the weeds all cheer, 'This is getting tough!'

The daisies chime in with a floral tune,
As the sun peeks out, 'Oh, it's afternoon!'
The cactus just pricks at its own little fun,
Saying, 'I'll win this game—when I'm 20 feet tall!'

In the Embrace of the Wild

In the garden, weeds are spry,
They dance beneath the summer sky.
But when I turn, and take a peek,
They giggle soft, oh what a leak.

The flowers boast, they wear their crowns,
While bugs parade in silly gowns.
I swear I saw a fern on stilts,
It tripped and fell, oh what a jilt!

Each tree has tales, they sway and creak,
Of squirrels who stole a cracker cheek.
In nature's realm, humor's alive,
Even the shyest shrub will thrive!

In laughter's arms, we find our bliss,
Among the branches, can't dismiss.
With roots that tangle and play around,
Life's a jest in the wild, unbound.

Secrets of the Understory

Beneath the leaves, a world unseen,
Where fungi dance, and critters preen.
A worm declares, with quite the flair,
"I'm just a noodle, without a care!"

The snails wear jackets, oh so bright,
As they glide home in the dead of night.
A beetle jokes with brazen glee,
"I'm just here for the company!"

Mushrooms peek from their cozy beds,
Whispering secrets, turning heads.
A spider spun a tale so sly,
"I'm just a web designer, oh my!"

Each earthy nook holds joys profound,
In soil's embrace, puns abound.
With laughter strong, and life a groove,
In nature's depths, we sway and move.

Where History Lies

Beneath the stones, ancestors snicker,
Histories told with a funny sticker.
Old roots entwined in tales so grand,
Of silly squirrels and a clumsy band.

The mossy plaques have stories to share,
Of frogs in tuxedos, beyond compare.
The wind carries whispers from times long gone,
"Did you hear about the bird who could yawn?"

Trees hold the laughter of ages past,
Of owls who hooted, but fell at last.
It's all a page in nature's tome,
Where even the rocks have made their home.

In every crack, a chuckle reverberates,
Life's punchlines weave, as history waits.
With humor rooted in every glance,
The past's a party, let's join the dance!

Frozen in Growth

In winter's grip, the plants wear frost,
While dreaming of sunshine, they feel lost.
But in their slumber, they plot and scheme,
To burst forth laughing, like a springtime dream.

Icicles dangle in a comedic way,
"Don't slip!" they shout - oh what a play!
The snowflakes swirl in dramatic flair,
While snowmen sit with their frozen stares.

The evergreens nod, wisdom in tow,
They share winter jokes about life in the snow.
"Just wait," they chuckle, "Till warmth hits us,
We'll blossom and giggle, don't make a fuss!"

Each frosty morn brings a breeze of cheer,
In nature's comedy, we cheer and jeer.
With roots in the ground, a silly show,
Where growth can be funny, just watch it glow!

Tales in the Twisted Wood

In the woods where the trees conspire,
Squirrels dance on a wire with desire.
Raccoons wear masks, they think they're the best,
Trying to steal snacks, oh what a quest!

Owls hoot and gossip, full of delight,
While mushrooms giggle, a funny sight.
The logs crack jokes, they're punny and wise,
Nature's comedy show, right before our eyes!

Bunnies hop in a silly parade,
Wearing tiny hats that they've homemade.
They trip on their ears and tumble about,
In this twisted wood, there's never a doubt!

So come take a stroll 'neath branches so grand,
Laughing with critters, you'll understand.
Nature's a jester, with a wink and a grin,
In this leafy kingdom, we're all born to win.

Nature's Haiku

Leaves whisper secrets,
A snail slips on a banana,
Nature's comic show.

Birds take flight, mid-laugh,
Dodging droppings from above,
Not their finest hour.

Rivers giggle soft,
Over rocks they tumble down,
Splashing all around.

Insects dance in light,
Twisting and turning with flair,
Nature's quirky beat.

Echoes of the Earth

The ground starts to shake, is it a joke?
Nope, just a bear that's learned to poke.
"Knock-Knock!" he roars, with a grin so wide,
"Mind if I join you? Let's take it outside!"

Mountains chuckle slow, in echoes profound,
As waterfalls slip and make giggling sounds.
The valleys join in with a cheeky shout,
"Keep it down up there! We're trying to chill out!"

Trees sway their heads, ruffling their hair,
"Who needs a barber? We're wild and free, we swear."
Leaves flutter down in a rustling cheer,
Nature's own laughter, so bright and clear.

So gather 'round friends, let's share in the fun,
With all of the critters, we're never outdone.
In echoes of joy, through the forest we roam,
Each laugh a reminder, we're never alone.

The Depths of Awareness

Under the soil, the worms hold a ball,
With radishes dressed in the finest of all.
They twirl and they spin, in dirt so divine,
"Who knew being underground could be this fine?"

The roots play charades, in the dark of the night,
While rocks roll their eyes, "You're not getting it right!"
With laughter they clamor, the mushrooms take flight,
In this underground realm, the mood's just right!

Fungi wear crowns, made of moss and of dew,
They chuckle and cheer, "You can join us too!"
Each hidden endeavor brings giggles to share,
In depths of awareness, we find joy in the air.

So dance in the dirt, let your spirit release,
Embrace all the quirks that make nature a feast.
For laughter's the root that connects us all,
In the depth of existence, we answer the call.

Shadows in the Darkened Grove

In the grove where shadows play,
Squirrels gossip about the day.
A raccoon with a hat so grand,
Claims he's king of this leafy land.

Mushrooms dance under the moon,
Fungi giggle to a tune.
The owls hoot, giving a wink,
As fireflies swirl and blink.

A gardener's spade, lost in the mist,
Whispers secrets that can't be missed.
The trees chuckle with branches swaying,
Roots below, still quietly playing.

In the shadows, tales unfold,
Of brash leaves that once were bold.
Invertebrates tell jokes so dry,
While beneath, the worms sigh and pry.

The Weight of Unseen Connections

A cactus stands all prickly and proud,
While a fern whispers softly, 'Hey, that's loud!'
They swap rumors through the soil's embrace,
Critiquing the moss's unkempt grace.

A bluebird and a beetle once met,
Swapped stories that they'd never forget.
The breeze tickled the branches above,
As roots shared secrets like old friends do love.

The soil grumbles of tales untold,
Of roots tying hearts strong and bold.
Every garden unearths its throng,
Where laughter and roots both belong.

Though hidden below, connections run deep,
Life's funny in shadows where secrets creep.
These quirks of nature hold joy, spry and bright,
As unseen messengers dance in the night.

Memories Woven in the Fibers

In tangled threads of earthy delight,
Sits a spider weaving memories tight.
An acorn dropped with a plop so loud,
    Plans a party beneath the cloud.

The ivy clings from olden days,
    Recalling tales of sunlit rays.
With laughter trapped in the bark's embrace,
    Funny echoes linger in the space.

Old roots remember the dance of rain,
    While curious critters come to feign.
When the dogwood starts to break into bloom,
    The whispers of history scatter the gloom.

In fibers deep, eccentricity thrives,
    As the soil giggles, comedy derives.
Life weaves together, blending the cheer,
    For every plant has its own funny sphere.

The Buried Stories of the Past

Beneath the earth lie stories so sly,
Of gnomes who giggled and told tales awry.
A shovel's chuckle, as it strikes the ground,
Unearths the laughter that's been around.

Old roots nestle, all tangled in cheer,
They reminisce while the worms lend an ear.
A stone's sharp retort keeps them all awake,
As shadows shuffle in the cool earth's bake.

The past wiggles with each passing breeze,
Tickling branches and whispering leaves.
The things they've seen in their long, winding quest,
Exchanging old jokes that never rest.

So dig a little deeper, revel in the fun,
Where buried stories weave, never on the run.
Every twist and turn shares its own song,
Roots chortle softly, 'This is where we belong!'

Shadows of the Ancients

In a garden of whispers, the trees tell a joke,
Their branches are creaking, they giggle, they croak.
Among ancient shadows, the flowers all laugh,
As the sunlight tickles the old weathered path.

The squirrels have secrets, they chatter with glee,
Plotting their acorns in wild jubilee.
A wise old raccoon, with a knowing glance,
Winks at the ferns and invites them to dance.

The moon is a comedian, with beams full of light,
Telling the night sky it's just a delight.
While owls hoot in chorus, with terrible puns,
The laughter echoes 'neath the light of the suns.

In the end, it's a riot, this life we all share,
Nature's a stand-up with jokes everywhere.
So next time you wander through shadows so deep,
Remember the guardians of giggles and keep!

The Buried Truth

Beneath a tall oak, a squirrel found gold,
Or so he believed, in his stories retold.
With acorn ambition, he dug up the ground,
Only to find a lost shoe, quite profound.

The worms had a meeting, their gossip was slick,
About buried treasure and dirty old tricks.
Finding some roots, they claimed it a win,
While the ants in their suits were wearing thin grins.

A hedgehog popped out, saying 'What's all the fuss?'
'It's only my breakfast, you all can't discuss!'
As laughter erupted, the soil turned brown,
With the truth in the digging and giggles renown.

So let's tip our hats to the chaos below,
Where the chortles of nature just steal all the show.
For the buried truth often hides in plain sight,
Wrapped in a riddle, with humor so bright!

In the Grip of Darkness

One night in the woods, the shadows took flight,
A raccoon with a mask thought it felt just right.
He swung from the branches, a mischief maker,
With moths as his audience, oh what a faker!

The owls held a party, but forgot the snacks,
They offered their wisdom and hooted some quacks.
While crickets in chorus sang songs of the night,
They cracked jokes about stars and their distant light.

Then came a wise fox with a trick up his sleeve,
'In twilight's embrace, I can easily deceive!'
He danced with the shadows, much to their dismay,
As the night rolled on, humor led the way.

In the grip of that darkness, joy found its way,
With laughter and folly, all fears went astray.
Remember this tale of the night's funny plight,
Where shadows and giggles forever unite!

Nature's Confessional

In a grove of confessions, the trees start to sigh,
They whisper of secrets while birds flutter by.
With humor aplenty, they air out their woes,
Sharing old stories of who stepped on whose toes.

The flowers have gossip, their petals all swayed,
About bees that forgot where their buzz was displayed.
While the grass grows taller, it nods its green head,
Laughing at daisies and wildflowers bred.

The wind plays a prank, tickling branches and leaves,
Making trees stumble, 'Oh, don't take your leaves!'
While critters all giggle at the forest's retort,
Nature's confessional was quite the report.

So when you stroll past with a smile on your face,
Remember the stories that thrive in this place.
For nature is funny; it tickles the soul,
In its vibrant confession, we all play a role!

The Language of Leaves

Whispers of green, they chuckle and sway,
Tickling the branches in bright ballet.
They gossip of sun, of rain's gentle tease,
In a dance of delight, as they rustle the breeze.

A leaf once said, 'I'm just here for fun!'
While trying to outshine the bright summer sun.
'You think you're so grand, with your very own shade?'
'But I'm just a leaf, here to play in this parade.'

With giggles, they twist, and they flick in the air,
A symphony of green, without any care.
They throw silly shapes, in a game of charades,
While squirrels get puzzled, with their leafy charades.

So next time you're walking through gardens of glee,
Remember the chatter, the green jubilee.
For leaves have their secrets, their fun to unveil,
In a world full of laughter, where nature won't fail.

Unseen Connections

In the underground, where the wild roots play,
A party exists that keeps boredom at bay.
'Hey neighbor, pass water!' the thirsty ones shout,
While all of the worms form a curious clout.

'Who knew we'd be friends through the dirt and the muck?'
Said one little root with a good bit of luck.
'We share our delights and our nutrients too,
It's a roots' revolution, can you hear our woohoo?'

The mushrooms stand guard, acting quirky and wise,
While sending weird signals, like nature's surprise.
'We can't see each other, but here's the fine snare,
Together we thrive, without needing fresh air!'

So cherish the links that you cannot see,
For life has its ways of snickering with glee.
In the quiet of soil, the funniest jest,
Is knowing you're part of this wild little fest.

Growth from Within

A seed once dreamed of what it could be,
Saying, 'I want to be tall, like that shade tree!'
It stretched and it wiggled, right under the ground,
'Oh please, just let me shoot up, I'm ready to bound!'

With the sunlight's first kiss, it poked at the sky,
But ended with branches that bobbed and awry.
'I wanted to be a grand cedar of note,
But look at me now, I'm a bush with a coat!'

'The real trick,' said a vine, 'is just having fun,
It's not how you grow, but how you are spun.
Twist and turn, make shapes that impress,
Embrace every wiggle, life's a funny mess!'

So laugh at your journey, wherever you stand,
Life's less about growing, more about the hand.
For every weird twist and each twisty little grin,
Is teaching you, darling, what growth is within!

The Weight of Existence

A cactus once sighed, 'Oh, what a tough gig,
With all this sharp armor, I just feel so big!'
'While others bask freely, I prick and I poke,
Not quite the belle of the ball, what a joke!'

The oak tree, so grand, with branches well-spread,
Grumbled, 'All this standing, it fills me with dread.
With squirrels and birds laying claims on my crown,
I'm basically a hotel, that keeps falling down!'

Meanwhile, the daisy rolled with laughter so loud,
'You think you've got problems? Stand tall in this crowd!

I barely survive with a bump and a shove,
While you, my dear friends, are just pining for love!'

So ponder your weight, and all that you bear,
For funny old nature has a quirky flair.
From prickly to lofty, we all have our plight,
Yet together we chuckle through life's loopy flight.

The Stillness of Entangled Existence

In a pot too small for my dreams,
I wiggle and squirm, or so it seems.
Like socks in a drawer, I can't escape,
My roots dance a jig, in a plastic cape.

I gaze at the sun with envy aflame,
While my neighbor's tree plays the growing game.
I shout at the sky, "Just give me some space!"
But my tangled friends find it hard to embrace.

With every leaf that tickles my face,
I wonder if I might win the race.
The dirt tells me jokes, it's quite absurd,
But laughter is green, and dreams go unheard.

So here I remain, in this comfy cell,
With thoughts taken hostage, oh what the hell!
If roots could roll eyes, I'd see them align,
In the stillness of life, we're all feeling fine.

Echoes of Resilience in the Dark.

In shadows where the soil is deep,
The whispers of the night start to creep.
I giggle with worms, oh what a jest,
Down here, we know how to have the best.

A thump in the night, what's that I hear?
A clumsy mole? Or just my own fear?
We crack up laughing at the funky sounds,
As echoes of resilience bounce all around.

The stars above, they twinkle and tease,
But down in the dark, there's a different breeze.
With roots intertwined like a funny dance,
We sway to the tunes of fate and chance.

Who needs the sun when we're having fun?
We'll start a rave, it's just begun!
For in this abyss where the soil goes stark,
We find our joy, echoing in the dark.

Whispers Beneath the Soil

Beneath the layers, secrets exchange,
Between sleepy roots—life feels so strange.
A gossip session with the grubs and bugs,
Tell all the tales of our dirt-bound hugs.

Each clump of earth, a story to share,
Of ants with dreams and worms with flair.
We chuckle at rocks, with their stony frowns,
For laughter and joy far outweigh the crowns.

When rain starts to fall, it's a splashy spree,
A muddy soirée just for us three.
We twirl in the gloom, like a wiggly rave,
In the whispers below, we're utterly brave.

So come join the dance, in shadows untold,
Where friendships bloom and adventures are bold.
In whispers we thrive, all snug in our ground,
For under the surface, true magic is found.

Tethered to the Earth

Stuck in this plot, I fret and I stew,
With earth on my roots, what can I do?
I dream of the clouds, but who needs the sky?
When you've got planted pals, oh me, oh my!

The neighbors all grumble about my size,
But I'm quirky and bold, just check out my eyes!
We trade our old stories, all tangled in glee,
As I throw all my weight just to shake free.

A thunderous thump and a laugh from above,
It's just Mr. Squirrel on his wild love!
He flits through the branches, so spry and so light,
While I'm stuck below in this grounded plight.

But I'm tethered in joy, with wiggles and cheer,
For earth's my domain, with friends ever near.
So let's raise a root, and dance 'round this turf,
In the laughter of dirt, we find our true worth.

Hidden Threads of Fate

In the garden of quirks, I found a sprout,
With socks on its leaves, it stood about.
It whispered of secrets, oh so bizarre,
Claiming to know where the lost socks are.

The daisies laughed, the worms chimed in,
They told me tales that made me grin.
Of fashion tips from the ants in a line,
Who wore little hats and danced just fine.

A tomato had dreams of being a star,
But worried too much about being too far.
It tried to roll over, but got stuck in the dirt,
And called for help with a comical hurt.

I sat there giggling, my tea in-hand,
In a world where veggies had bands so grand.
With roots so tangled and stories to share,
Life's antics sprouted everywhere we dare.

Echoes in the Underbrush

In the thicket, a rabbit wore shades of flair,
Sipping on smoothies, with nary a care.
"Why hop when you can chill?" it declared with a boast,
As onlookers chuckled, and he raised a toast.

A raccoon nearby, with a shiny old fork,
Was planning to host the first dinner and cork.
He waved to the squirrels, and to my surprise,
They came dressed in tuxes, all ready to rise!

The crickets provided a symphonic cheer,
As fireflies twinkled, both far and near.
A waltz in the woods, not a care in the world,
As laughter and mischief around us unfurled.

So gather your friends, in the shadowy glen,
For the party's just starting; let's do it again!
With snacks made of acorns, and laughter to share,
Echoes of joy dance, with naught but a flare.

Beneath the Surface

Underneath the pond, where the frogs like to sing,
Lies a world where the fish wear a crown made of bling.
They argued about styles, from stripes to the dots,
While turtles played chess with their slow, silly thoughts.

One fish claimed to swim with the utmost finesse,
While tripping on algae, it caused quite a mess.
The lily pads giggled, as they floated in pride,
For they knew the secrets of guests they'd supplied.

The dragonflies danced with a dazzling grace,
Challenging beetles to a quick-muddy race.
Amidst all the chaos, a catfish sat still,
With dreams of a life that involved a big thrill.

So chuckle at whimsy, beneath scenic waves,
For the pond holds the laughter, the laughs that it saves.
A world beyond bubbles, where friendships ignite,
And tales from the depths bring delight to the night.

Solace in the Stillness

In the quiet of dusk, the hedgehog reclined,
With dreams of grand journeys, it felt rather aligned.
It packed up a snack, then sat down to think,
About launching a ship with a bottle of ink.

Nearby, a wise owl was honing its craft,
Writing novels of mischief with a hint of a laugh.
Beneath a thick branch, the shadows would play,
As critters gathered 'round to hear what they'd say.

A mouse with a pencil drew maps on the ground,
Of cheese-filled adventures that once had been found.
With giggles and snickers, the night became bright,
As laughter erupted, bringing comfort and light.

So join in the stillness, let chuckles unfold,
For each whispered story brings warmth to the cold.
In solace, we gather to share and to scheme,
Creating our tales, like a wild, joyful dream.

Landscapes of Longing

In fields of grass where dreams are shy,
A chicken dances, oh my, oh my!
With flip-flops made of muddy clay,
It struts around like it's the mainstay.

The daisies giggle as they sway,
While clouds debate the price of hay.
A squirrel dons a tiny hat,
And scolds the flowers for being flat.

The river babbles, 'What's your plan?'
As fish play cards with a well-read man.
A butterfly joins the jamboree,
While ants form lines for their tea party.

In this odd place where wishes roam,
You'll find that bizarre is truly home.
So pucker up, give fate a spin,
And laugh out loud, let the fun begin!

The Weight of the World Above

The sky hangs low, it's feeling blue,
With clouds that frown, what can we do?
A giraffe wears boots to reach the sun,
While kangaroos just want to run.

The eagles argue over whose turn,
To soar and glide, their hearts all yearn.
A pancake flipped becomes a kite,
Sailing away in glutenous flight.

The sun jokes, 'Why don't you all chill?'
While drizzle brings a window sill.
The moon sighs softly, 'Lighten up,
These clouds need jokes, not coffee cups!'

Yet through the gloom, a laugh breaks free,
As gravity pulls them back—teehee!
So here we stand, with antics galore,
Lifting the weight, we can't ignore!

In the Heart of the Forest

In the heart of the woods, a dance unfolds,
Where trees wear tutus and stories are told.
A raccoon recites a Shakespeare play,
While owls debate the best serve for prey.

The mushrooms giggle under their hats,
Each step a squishy greeting from rats.
A fox does a jig on a fallen log,
While frogs jump high to the beat of a fog.

The pine cones cheer for the tallest tree,
With tiny squirrels shouting, 'Look at me!'
A breeze passes by with a ticklish tease,
Sending the leaves into fits of wheeze.

So in this glade of woodland flair,
Joy wraps around like a cozy chair.
With laughter echoing, you'll find,
That nature knows how to be kind!

The Longing for Light

A snail once dreamed of flying high,
With glittery wings and cake in the sky.
It plotted out how to become a star,
With gummy bears rolled up in a car.

The moon winked down with an airy grin,
'Just take your time; you'll surely win!'
But the stars laughed so loud they fell,
Creating a ruckus, a bright show-and-tell.

Down on Earth, a worm moped and sighed,
'Why can't I loop-de-loop and glide?'
But his neighbor, a bee, buzzed back with cheer,
'Just dance in the sun; we love you here!'

So soon the day brought a gleam to the ground,
With laughter and light all dancing around.
For in the glow of a coffee-filled day,
Longings for light simply fade away!

The Path Beneath My Feet

I stumbled on a vine so neat,
It danced around my wandering feet.
A frog in a tie said, "Mind the leap!"
I grinned and followed, not losing sleep.

The squirrels took note of my clumsy show,
They chattered and laughed, oh what a foe!
I stepped on a beetle, it shouted, "Hey!"
Nature's comedy in a bright display.

With every step, I felt more spry,
An acorn whispered, "Come give it a try!"
I tripped on a root—oh, what a spree!
My dance with the earth, pure ecstasy.

The ground below is quite the tease,
It tickles my toes in the summer breeze.
So as I wander, let laughter be,
The path beneath is wild and free.

Nature's Hidden Dialogues

In the garden, the gnomes conspire,
They plot and plan with wild desire.
A daffodil told a rose with glee,
"Let's trick the weeds and dance for tea!"

The worms play poker, dirt-smudged and sly,
A beetle rolls dice, oh my, oh my!
The daisies gossip between shy blooms,
Covert operations in leafy rooms.

Beneath the branches, whispers abound,
The trees ink secrets in soft, green sound.
A squirrel's grand plans for autumn came,
"I'll store more nuts, I'll win this game!"

And thus the world spins, a funny affair,
With critters chatting and banters to share.
In nature's realm, humor's the key,
To laughter and joy, come play with me!

Whispers of the Wild

In the forest, the whispers flow,
A raccoon mumbles, "Where'd my snack go?"
The owls chuckle, oh how they preen,
At wily plans they've all seen.

The brook gurgles jokes, slippery and spry,
While trees sway gently, reaching for the sky.
"I'm taller than you!" the pine tree boasts,
While the maple rolls eyes, its bark a toast.

A laugh from the hedgehog, snug in his ball,
"I'll breakdance now, watch me enthrall!"
The wild is buzzing with jokes and cheer,
Even the rocks seem to grin ear to ear.

As night falls softly, stars start to play,
The critters gather for a nightly ballet.
It's a show of nature's own silly styles,
With giggles and grins across the miles.

Treetops and Tendrils

Atop the trees, the branches sway,
Laughter erupts in a playful fray.
The vines, they giggle, tickling the sky,
"Swinging with clouds? Give it a try!"

The squirrels discuss their latest dive,
"Who jumped higher? It's how we thrive!"
While leaves rustle secrets, bold and bright,
"I'll wave to the moon, see, what a sight!"

The air is thick with fun and delight,
As blossoms sway in the soft twilight.
A wandering breeze pulls laughter near,
Whispering tales that only it can hear.

With tendrils curling, they weave a dance,
Nature's fun, a whimsical prance.
So climb with me, in a world so sweet,
In treetops high, let laughter meet!

www.ingramcontent.com/pod-product-compliance
Lightning Source LLC
Chambersburg PA
CBHW072127070526
44585CB00016B/1562